WALDEN

THEN & NOW

An Alphabetical Tour of
Henry Thoreau's Pond

Michael McCurdy

﹋ Charlesbridge

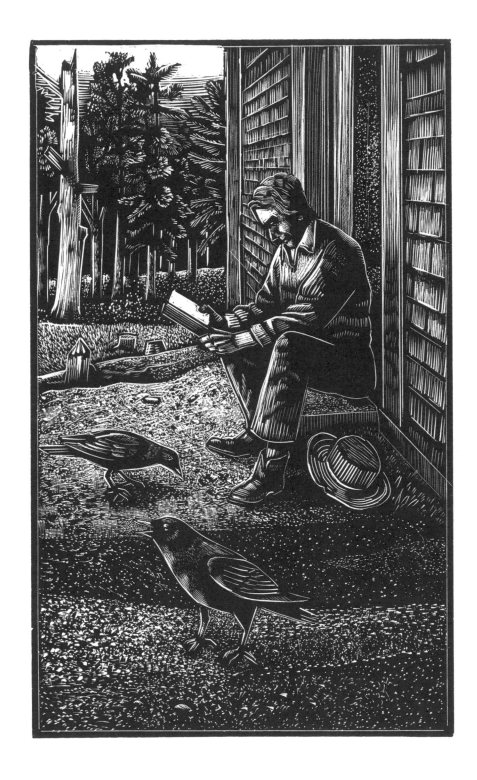

Who was Henry David Thoreau? Who is Michael McCurdy?

One was a man of nature, and one is a man of art. Although they are separated in time by more than a century, both of these New England men share a passion for preserving the natural world. Would they have liked each other? Probably. There's no doubt they would have admired each other's work.

Henry David Thoreau's book *Walden*, published in 1854, is a tribute to Mother Nature and the wildlife community of one particular pond. In the book you are holding, Michael McCurdy pays tribute to this historic place with dramatic images of its creatures and charm.

Why should young readers today know Henry's name? He was a man of all seasons: an author, a naturalist, a philosopher, an abolitionist (someone who opposed slavery), and most of all, a man who believed in simple living. His writings on nature laid the groundwork for today's environmental movement. Henry was "green" long before conservation became a world concern. Of all of his writings, *Walden* has had the most influence, and it is considered an American classic.

Long a fan of Michael's wood engravings, I was privileged to interview him for a book on children's illustrators. That lunch date became the start of a friendship. While I was working on an article about ABC books, which included Michael's *A Sailor's Alphabet*, an idea flickered: Michael should do a new alphabet book! His interest in Henry became the obvious link, and here is the beautiful result.

Like bees to pollen and crows to corn, both men were drawn to nature. Henry David Thoreau enriched the world by sharing its marvels. Michael McCurdy enriches books with his marvelous art. A unique symbiosis, then and now.

Julie Cummins, *Summer 2009*

A

is for the angry ants that Henry once saw battling.

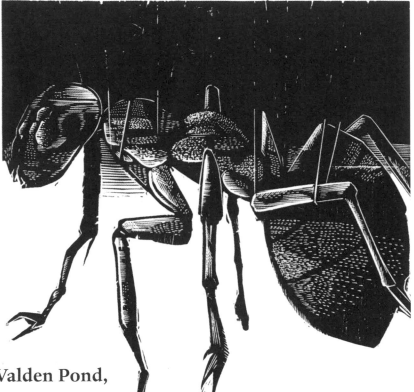

While Henry was living at Walden Pond, he saw black and red ants fighting. The ants haven't changed from Henry's time—they still fight one another. What's different is that in our time they have a greater chance of being stepped upon by a human. After all, the population of Concord in 1847 was about two thousand. Today there are more than sixteen thousand people in the town.

B

is for the bean field in which noisy crows were prattling.

Henry proudly reports in *Walden* that he cultivated some seven miles' worth of beans! He ate some of the beans he grew, but he sold most of them. Today most people go to the supermarket to buy beans, and fortunately there are no crows in the shopping aisles!

C
is for the cabin Henry built with his own hands.

Henry could do just about anything he put his mind to. He dug his cellar by hand, for example, although he needed additional help to raise the cabin's framework. Henry took wooden boards from an abandoned shanty on the opposite shore of the pond and used them for his own cabin. He also shingled the cabin, plastered its walls inside, and built a chimney. He completed the work in time to have a sturdy, warm home by the time winter came. A replica of Henry's cabin now stands at Walden Pond.

 **is for the dogs that roamed the winter woods in bands.**

In 1847 dogs roamed more freely than they do now. Most were put to work on the family farm, with few opportunities to be the pampered pets many dogs are today. The dogs Henry saw in the woods were mostly hounds, the ancestors of today's foxhounds and beagles. One of the most popular dogs of today, the golden retriever, would have been unknown to Henry because this breed wasn't found in America until early in the twentieth century.

E is for the eagle that flew high above the pond.

In Henry's time bald eagles were fair game for hunters. By the middle of the twentieth century, hunting, poaching, and the effects of dangerous pesticides had made the American bald eagle an endangered species. Fortunately the eagle population has increased dramatically since then. This comeback of America's national bird has been the result of our government's protection of the eagle from hunting and poaching, as well as bans on some of the most harmful pesticides.

 **is for the wooden flute that Henry played upon.**

Henry enjoyed playing his wooden flute while drifting slowly on Walden Pond in his rowboat, searching for fish for supper. Henry's flute was of a common sort, based on Irish and English models. In 1847, the year Henry stopped living at Walden Pond, the first metal cylinder flutes were made in Europe by Theobald Boehm.

G is for returning geese that made his spirits soar.

Winters were colder in Henry's time, and nearly all geese migrated to Mexico. Henry was cheered by their return in the spring, since it meant warmer weather was on its way. Canada geese of today seem less interested in flying south, choosing instead to feast on leftover grains and seeds found on snowless fields. Perhaps this is one more effect of rising temperatures around the globe.

H

is for the hare that thumped beneath the cabin floor.

Every morning upon rising from sleep, Henry would hear the "thump, thump, thump" of a hare scurrying for safety under his floorboards, bumping her head as she ran. The hare had made her home beneath the floor, but in her fright thought it wise to leave for the day when she heard Henry's footsteps above her.

I is for the winter ice that made the pond like stone.

In Henry's day there were no electric refrigerators for preserving food. Meat was usually smoked or packed in salt. Ice was also used to keep foods from spoiling. In winter Henry watched workmen take tons of ice from the pond. Using special saws, they cut the ice into blocks and packed it in straw and sawdust. The ice needed to remain solid for the long journey by ship to such faraway places as New Orleans and Singapore.

J

J is for the joy he felt at being all alone.

Henry was a friendly man who enjoyed talking with all kinds of people—but he also loved being by himself. In his cabin on Walden Pond, he felt at home with the birds, foxes, and other creatures in the woods. Today it would be hard to be alone at Walden Pond: nearly six hundred thousand people visit the pond every year.

K is for the kindling split as part of daily chores.

Henry had to split wood to burn for warmth in the winter. He wasn't the only one using Walden's trees. As early as 1859, Henry complained in his journal about the deforestation (cutting down of trees) at Walden in the years since he had left, and by 1922 most of the trees at Walden were gone. Today, thanks to new plantings and other conservation efforts by people and local governments, the woods around the pond are again filled with pine, oak, and hickory trees.

L

is for the loon that dove away from Henry's oars.

One October day while Henry was rowing on Walden Pond, a mischievous loon taunted him from the middle of the pond. The loon then dove out of sight into the deep water, returning to the surface much later, even farther from Henry's busy oars. Henry never did get close to the loon, who continued to heckle him with its strange and haunting laughter—always from the safety of the middle of the pond.

M is for the little mouse that ran up Henry's trousers.

Henry's favorite pet was a mouse that would eat the crumbs that fell from Henry's sandwich. The mouse would even scramble up and down Henry's clothes and take cheese from his hand! Today most people would be upset to find a mouse in their house, but Henry felt he shared his home with all of nature.

N is for the nighthawk that swooped low above the bowers.

The "common nighthawk" is not so common today. This bird, so plentiful in Henry's time, has experienced a noticeable decline in numbers since the 1970s. Henry loved watching nighthawks circle and dive—tumbling about in the air and then suddenly descending toward the treetops with a loud whoosh!

O is for the owls that called to Henry in the night.

Henry loved hearing the soft cries of the barred owl—"hoo hoo hoo, hooer hoo"—and the louder cry of the screech owl. The screech owl's hoots filled the night air, sometimes sounding like "*Oh-o-o-o-o that I never had been bor-r-r-r-n!*" In some areas you can still hear owls hooting at night, with calls that are scary to some but comforting to others.

**P** is for the pickerel that gave fishermen delight.

Henry's pond never had great quantities of fish. Henry caught shiners, chivins, roach, very few breams, and some eels, but pickerel was the most plentiful fish in the pond. In winter, fishermen would walk from town to cut a hole in the ice and drop their lines, hoping for a catch. Fishing is still allowed in Walden Pond today.

 **is for the quiet peace that Henry gladly found.**

The woods around Henry's cabin were never silent, but to Henry the sounds of the pond were a welcome change from the bustle of town. He loved listening to the calls of the birds and the splashes in the pond. He even enjoyed the distant sound of church bells from nearby towns. Today Walden Pond is tucked behind a highway, where thousands of commuters and vacationers drive every day. Visitors can still hear the birds and other Walden animals, but they can also hear the cars whizzing by.

R is for the railroad that brought the train's loud sound.

Henry didn't like the new Fitchburg Railroad and its noise. He said the train's whistle reminded him of a screaming hawk flying over a farmer's yard. He was also disturbed by the large amount of smoke that the locomotive produced. Even so, Henry used the railroad tracks as his highway to and from town, avoiding the times when he knew this wouldn't be safe. A train still goes by the pond on the same tracks, but there are no more lumps of coal for children to collect for fuel, as they did in Henry's time.

S is for the song sparrow that sang a cheerful tune.

It's more than likely that the first birds of spring, which Henry called song sparrows, were the field sparrows of today. Perhaps if you are really quiet, you too might hear the same song Henry heard many years ago coming from the fields: *"olit, olit, olit-chip, chip, chip, che char-che wiss, wiss, wiss."*

T is for the thrashers that stole farmers' seeds too soon.

The brown thrasher is declining in our own time. But in Henry's day there must have been a good number of these birds, which forage on the ground and eat seeds planted by farmers before the seeds can sprout. Thrashers also sleep on the ground, hiding in thickly constructed tangles of shrubs, leaves, and twigs, to keep them safe from marauders.

U is for Ursa Major, the great big starry bear.

Henry was very familiar with the constellations in the
night sky, which form part of our Milky Way. The Great
Bear is made up of more than fifty visible stars,
including the Big Dipper, which is formed by seven of
these stars. Real bears in Henry's time had nearly been
hunted to extinction. But today the black bear is back—
sometimes, unfortunately, in human habitats. This is
bad news for the bears, as people tend to view them as
a nuisance or are afraid of them.

V is for the visitors to Henry's cabin lair.

Henry did not live a true hermit's life by the edge of Walden Pond. Almost daily he walked the railroad tracks to town to gather the latest news and to do errands. But Henry also had many curious visitors who came out from Concord to see how this strange man was doing. Many children also stopped by, and Henry shared with them the secrets of the woods he knew so well. Today hundreds of thousands of visitors come to Walden Pond to swim, hike, fish, snowshoe—and often, to learn more about Henry.

W
is for the woodchopper who worked in summertime.

Henry became friends with a local woodchopper with whom he shared laughter and good conversation in summer and winter. Most wood-choppers, though, preferred to work just in the cold months. There were no annoying mosquitoes, horseflies, or deerflies in winter, and the wood could be more easily dragged across frozen, snow-covered ground than through the summer woods. Today the woods around Walden Pond are protected from woodchopping and further development, as people work to conserve the pond's natural landscape.

 **X** is for the unknown word we'd need for a good rhyme.

There was nothing at Walden Pond beginning with the rare letter *X*. Perhaps if Henry had known that there would someday be an alphabet book based on his days at Walden, he might have brought a xylophone to play, or a book by the ancient Greek writer Xenophon!

Y is for the yellow moon that bathes the pond in light.

One unchanging thing from Henry's time to ours has been the moon. Just imagine: every seeing human who has grown up on our Mother Earth has looked at the same moon you have looked at—and that includes Henry David Thoreau. Henry was surely as fascinated by the big shiny orb hanging in the sky as we are today.

 **is for the cooling zephyr on a summer night.**

A zephyr is a gentle breeze from the west. Henry liked to float in his boat on the pond sometimes, drifting wherever the zephyr took him. The zephyr must have offered great relief to Henry and the other citizens of Concord during New England's humid summer days—just as it still does today.

Source Notes

The references below show you some of the paragraphs in *Walden* where Henry mentions the things described in this book. These are not the only places where ants or beans or geese are mentioned, but they give you an idea of the way Henry wrote and thought about nature.

ANTS "I observed two large ants, the one red, the other much larger, nearly half an inch long, and black, fiercely contending with one another." (Chapter 12, paragraph 12)

BEANS "Meanwhile my beans, the length of whose rows, added together, was seven miles already planted, were impatient to be hoed." (Chapter 7, paragraph 1)

CABIN "I dug my cellar in the side of a hill sloping to the south." "I laid the foundation of a chimney at one end, bringing two cartloads of stones up the hill from the pond in my arms." (Chapter 1, section C, paragraphs 23 and 24)

DOGS "I sometimes heard a pack of hounds threading all the woods with hounding cry and yelp." (Chapter 15, paragraph 9)

EAGLE "An old man who used to frequent this pond nearly sixty years ago . . . tells me that in those days . . . there were many eagles about it." (Chapter 9, section B, paragraph 6)

FLUTE "In warm evenings I frequently sat in the boat playing the flute." (Chapter 9, section A, paragraph 3)

GEESE "Night after night the geese came lumbering in the dark with a clangor and a whistling of wings." (Chapter 13, paragraph 12)

HARE "One [hare] had her form under my house all winter . . . and she startled me each morning by her hasty departure when I began to stir—thump, thump, thump, striking her head against the floor timbers in her hurry." (Chapter 15, paragraph 14)

ICE "While yet it is cold January, and snow and ice are thick and solid, the prudent landlord comes from the village to get ice." (Chapter 16, paragraph 16)

JOY "I find it wholesome to be alone the greater part of the time. . . . I love to be alone. I never found the companion that was so companionable as solitude." (Chapter 5, paragraph 12)

KINDLING "I had an old axe . . . with which . . . I played about the stumps which I had got out of my bean-field. . . . They warmed me twice—once while I was splitting them, and again when they were on the fire, so that no fuel could give out more heat." (Chapter 13, paragraph 15)

LOON "In the fall the loon . . . came, as usual . . . making the woods ring with his wild laughter before I had risen." (Chapter 12, paragraph 16)

MOUSE "One of these [mice] would come out regularly at lunch time and pick up the crumbs at my feet. It . . . soon became quite familiar, and would run over my shoes and up my clothes." (Chapter 12, paragraph 9)

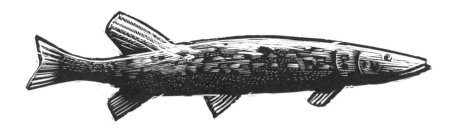

NIGHTHAWK "The night-hawk circled overhead in the sunny afternoons." (Chapter 7, paragraph 6)

OWLS "When other birds are still, the screech owls take up the strain. . . . *Oh-o-o-o-o that I never had been bor-r-r-n!* sighs one on this side of the pond. . . . Then—*that I never had been bor-r-r-n!* echoes another on the farther side." (Chapter 4, paragraph 18)

PICKEREL "Ah, the pickerel of Walden! . . . I am always surprised by their rare beauty." (Chapter 16, paragraph 5)

QUIET "I sat in my sunny doorway from sunrise till noon . . . in undisturbed solitude and stillness, while the birds sing around or flitted noiseless through the house." (Chapter 4, paragraph 2)

RAILROAD "The Fitchburg Railroad touches the pond about a hundred rods south of where I dwell. I usually go to the village along its causeway." "The whistle of the locomotive penetrates my woods summer and winter." (Chapter 4, paragraphs 6 and 7)

SONG SPARROW "I hear a song sparrow singing from the bushes on the shore—*olit, olit, olit-chip, chip, chip, che char-che wiss, wiss, wiss.*" (Chapter 17, paragraph 14)

THRASHERS "Near at hand, upon the topmost spray of a birch, sings the brown thrasher. . . . While you are planting the seed, he cries—'Drop it, drop it—cover it up, cover it up—pull it up, pull it up, pull it up.'" (Chapter 7, paragraph 5)

URSA MAJOR "How far apart, think you, dwell the two most distant inhabitants of yonder star . . . ? Why should I feel lonely? is not our planet in the Milky Way?" (Chapter 5, paragraph 5)

VISITORS "I had more visitors while I lived in the woods than at any other period in my life." "Girls and boys and young women generally seemed glad to be in the woods. They looked in the pond and at the flowers, and improved their time." (Chapter 6, paragraphs 7 and 17)

WOODCHOPPER "Sometimes I saw him at his work in the woods, felling trees, and he would greet me with a laugh of inexpressible satisfaction." (Chapter 6, paragraph 10)

XENOPHON "The adventurous student will always study classics, in whatever language they may be written and however ancient they may be. For what are the classics but the noblest recorded thoughts of man?" (Chapter 3, paragraph 3)

YELLOW MOON "At midnight, when there was a moon, I sometimes met with hounds in my path prowling about the woods." (Chapter 15, paragraph 12)

ZEPHYR "I have spent many an hour, when I was younger, floating over [the pond's] surface as the zephyr willed." (Chapter 9, section B, paragraph 7)

To my wife, Deborah—
and to our children, Heather and Mark,
with whom we shared many happy hours
on the shores of Walden Pond.

Text copyright © 2010 by Michael McCurdy

Ant illustration on page 4 copyright © 1981 by Michael McCurdy. Originally appeared in *Everything That Has Been Shall Be Again: The Reincarnation Fables of John Gilgun*, published by The Bieler Press, Marina del Rey, California. Used with permission.

Eagle illustration on page 8 copyright © 1987 by Michael McCurdy. Originally appeared in *JFK Remembered* by Arthur Schlesinger, published by Thornwillow Press, Newburgh, New York. Used with permission.

Hare illustration on page 11 copyright © 2005 by Michael McCurdy. Originally appeared in *Tales of Adam* by Daniel Quinn, published by Steerforth Press of Hanover, New Hampshire. Used with permission.

Owl illustration on page 18 copyright © 1986 by Michael McCurdy. Originally appeared in *The Owl Scatterer* by Howard Norman, published by the Atlantic Monthly Press, New York. Used with permission.

All other illustrations copyright © 2004 by Michael McCurdy. Originally appeared in the 150th anniversary edition of *Walden*, published by Shambhala Publications, Inc., Boston. Reprinted with permission of the publisher.

All rights reserved, including the right of reproduction in whole or in part in any form. Charlesbridge and colophon are registered trademarks of Charlesbridge Publishing, Inc.

Published by Charlesbridge
85 Main Street
Watertown, MA 02472
(617) 926-0329
www.charlesbridge.com

LIBRARY OF CONGRESS CATALOGING-IN-PUBLICATION DATA
McCurdy, Michael.
  Walden then & now : an alphabetical tour of Henry Thoreau's pond / Michael McCurdy.
     p. cm.
  ISBN 978-1-58089-253-7 (reinforced for library use)
1. Thoreau, Henry David, 1817–1862—Homes and haunts—Massachusetts—Walden Woods—Juvenile literature.
2. Thoreau, Henry David, 1817–1862. Walden—Juvenile literature. 3. Natural history—Massachusetts—Walden Woods—Juvenile literature. 4. Walden Woods (Mass.)—Juvenile literature. 5. Alphabet books. I. Title. II. Title: Walden then and now.
PS3053.M385 2010
818'.309 [B 22]   2009026645

Printed in China
(hc) 10 9 8 7 6 5 4 3 2 1

Illustrations are wood engravings
Display type and text type set in Dante
Color separations by Chroma Graphics
Printed and bound February 2010 by Jade Productions in Heyuan, Guangdong, China
Production supervision by Brian G. Walker
Designed by Susan Mallory Sherman

Michael McCurdy is the author and illustrator of *An Algonquian Year, Hannah's Farm,* and *Trapped in the Ice.* He is also the illustrator of more than 200 books for adults and children, including *The Founders: The 39 Stories Behind the Constitution* and *The Train They Call the City of New Orleans.* He lives in Springfield, Massachusetts, with his wife, Deborah.